MW00907251

Merrie Carlisle and poems of tradition

Hugh Falconer

Nabu Public Domain Reprints:

You are holding a reproduction of an original work published before 1923 that is in the public domain in the United States of America, and possibly other countries. You may freely copy and distribute this work as no entity (individual or corporate) has a copyright on the body of the work. This book may contain prior copyright references, and library stamps (as most of these works were scanned from library copies). These have been scanned and retained as part of the historical artifact.

This book may have occasional imperfections such as missing or blurred pages, poor pictures, errant marks, etc. that were either part of the original artifact, or were introduced by the scanning process. We believe this work is culturally important, and despite the imperfections, have elected to bring it back into print as part of our continuing commitment to the preservation of printed works worldwide. We appreciate your understanding of the imperfections in the preservation process, and hope you enjoy this valuable book.

MERRIE CARLISLE

AND

POEMS OF TRADITION

BY

HUGH FALCONER, B.D.

Minister of the Presbyterian Church of England, Carlisle ;
Author of "The Maid of Shulam" and "The Unfinished Symphony."

Second Edition Revised.

CARLISLE:
CHAS. THURNAM & SONS, 11 ENGLISH STREET.
1914.

First Edition, December, 1913.

Second Edition, January, 1914.

TRADE AGENTS—

LONDON: SIMPKIN, MARSHALL & CO., LTD.

EDINBURGH & GLASGOW: IOHN MENZIES & CO., LTD

Ever yours truly

Hugh Falconer

To

The Congregation at Carlisle,

and

The Friends, Physicians, and Nurses,

whose kindness has been so unfailing

during his Protracted Illness,

the Writer

Gratefully offers this Handful of Flowers

from a Hospital Garden.

CONTENTS.

———

LIST OF ILLUSTRATIONS.

l

PROLOGUS GALEATUS.

This little volume may need a "helmeted prologue" to vindicate its publication.

It is printed in the hope that it may serve the great cause of local patriotism. In two recent lectures on the "value of local tradition" the writer ventured to recite to large popular audiences some of the following pieces, with their prose prefaces. He was surprised by the enthusiasm evoked, by a request for publication, and even by a remonstrance that more ballads had not been given. An illustrated version of one piece was printed as a set of picture post cards, and 18,000 copies have been sold. It then occurred to him that singers in the 20th century might do well on occasion, like the old minstrels, to recite their verses to the people, who seem to cherish a great liking for verse, sung or spoken—provided the subject awaken their interest. Also that a brief record of his experience might be of service to some reader whose proper vocation, unlike that of the writer, is poetry.

It may be urged that local tradition has only a limited appeal. But the universal may shine through the particular, and the ideal through the concrete instance. Was it not said of old, " History is but Philosophy teaching by examples "? Or it may be said that the poet should help people, and especially young folk, to " contemplate the spectacle of life with appropriate emotions " as it is lived at present, or will be in the near future, rather than as it was in the past. But they will best understand and serve their own generation—at home and overseas—whose sympathetic imagination has first been exercised on the records of their own countryside, and the vividly coloured experience of their forbears. Happily, from its wealth of historic monuments, no country is better fitted than our own to develop in the citizens of the future that power of the mind to project itself into the consciousness of others, and see life as they see it, which is the secret of good manners and worthy social service.

Is not the time at hand when classical figures as poetic symbols shall abdicate, letting familiar typical national figures reign in their stead? Is not Mary, Queen of Scots, as symbolical a tragic heroine as Iphigenia or Œnone? A Cromwell or a Nelson as poetic a hero as Achilles or Hector? Raleigh or Livingstone as typical a wanderer as Jason or Ulysses? Robert Burns as ideal a lyrist as Sappho or Tyrtæus? The devotion of our poets in time past to classical themes—as if these alone embodied the ideal and universal—has rendered poetry caviare to the general. A change of poetic symbols from the unknown to the familiar might mean much for the interest of the democracy in poetry. At any rate there is no reason why poetry should not appeal to the million as well as to the cultured few. If they but read aright the signs of our time, our younger poets should soon come into their kingdom. Let them don their singing robes for the people, not for a small exclusive coterie. Is it not foolish of Church and State to ignore the measureless potencies of social service wrapped up in popular song? Is not one half of the Old Testament poetry? And in the light of this fact, is it not surprising that our British Church history, with its stirring episodes, and above all the romance of the last century of Missions, has not been sung into the popular heart, but still remains, poetically speaking, virgin soil?

To the pieces on local tradition the writer adds some others indicating more definitely his attitude to life, and suggesting, however brokenly, some aspects of that supreme interpreter of experience—our greatest tradition and heritage—the Christian evangel of the most blessed God. The " helmeted prologue," then, may perhaps vindicate this book as the plea of a provincial voice that poets, as of old, sing and recite their verse to the people, not to a clique, and that due recognition of the exceeding value of tradition—local, national, Christian—be made by a democratic age, which looks with infectious eagerness to the future, and has set its hand in earnest to the titanic task of social reconstruction.

In the first section of this volume some of the pieces were originally composed in the Scots dialect, but these have been modified to save the reader from the distraction of footnotes explaining the vernacular. In the second section the texts were an afterthought. The pieces were written on some spontaneous impulse and then found susceptible of Scripture texts, as indeed are all the poems in both sections. Unconsciously, the writer's outlook has been coloured by the measure of his apprehension of the Christian view. In simple truth, apart from that, he could make nothing of life and death at all, but would be utterly in the dark, and driven to despair of his brother-men and himself. The Evangel is his all. But it is infinite.

The writer's thanks are due to the Rev. A. E. Bloxsome Day, D.D., for the photograph of the fourteenth century house in King's Arms Lane, now printed for the first time; to the Rev. David Connor for the use of his plates of the Bewcastle Cross; to the Rev. J. E. Mc.Vittie, for the photograph of Hexham Abbey; to J. P. D.

i

Wheatley, Esq., for permission to reproduce various photographs relating to Prince Charlie; to Messrs. J. Russell & Sons for permission to use their portrait of the writer; to Messrs. Gibson, of Hexham, and Messrs. Nicholson & Cartner, of Carlisle, for photographs of Dilston Castle, Gilnockie Tower, the Popping Stone, and the Sauceries; to his dear friend Canon Rawnsley for constant interest and valuable suggestions; and to Revs. J. Gilfillan, G. J. Goodman, and J. E. Falconer for kind help in correcting proofs.
What a deal of kindness there is in the world! The writer puts on record this testimony (probably his last), that as a traveller from boyhood in many lands, he has found the kindness of his brother-men absolutely unfailing, and their varied talent passing wonderful. He is sorry to leave them so soon. God bless them all. Could the vast kindliness of the human heart but be focussed somehow on life, half. of the ills that afflict long-suffering mankind— tackled concertedly and in God's name—would vanish like vapour.

MERRIE CARLISLE.

The epithet " merrie " denotes the celebrity of
the City in the olden time for deeds of warlike daring
that still stir the blood like the sound of a trumpet.
Especially for gallant defence was Carlisle famous,
and in the long list of her besiegers are the names of
William the Lion, Alexander II, the Earl of Buchan,
Wallace, Bruce, Douglas, Cromwell, Lesly, and the
Duke of Cumberland. Among her muniments is a
charter, dating from 1314, whose initial letter vividly
portrays the successful defence of the City by Andrew
de Harcla, the governor, against King Robert the
Bruce, fresh from his triumph at Bannockburn, and
eager to avenge the cruel execution of his brothers
Thomas and Edward, at Carlisle, in the last year of
Edward I.   In the annals of Carlisle the most
romantic episodes are the residence of Mary, Queen
of Scots, in the castle, during May and June, 1568;

the rescue from one of the castle dungeons of
Kinmont Willie, the dreaded Scots freebooter, by
" bold Buccleuch " his Warden, and the young bloods
of the clan Scott, in April 1596, when " keen
Scrope " was the English Warden; and the triumphal
entrance of " Bonnie Prince Charlie " in November
1745, on a white charger, and preceded by a hundred
pipers.

In Roman times Carlisle was an important
military base, and later an ecclesiastical centre; but
under the Danes it became a waste, and for several
centuries was merely a ruinous bit of British Strath-
clyde. " Carlisle and the district round it," says
Mr. Freeman, " do not figure in the Domesday Book
Survey." In the Saxon Chronicle, under date
A.D. 1092, is this brief significant entry :—" In this
year the King William, with a large army, went
north to Carlisle, and drove out Dolphin that before
governed the land, and set his own men in the castle,
and then returned hither southward. And a vast
number of rustic people with wives and with
cattle, he sent thither to dwell there in order to till
the land." In the middle of the 12th century King
David of Scotland held court in the Border City,
received papal legates, and knighted Prince Henry
of England. He died in Carlisle in 1153. Under
King Edward I, in the first decade of the 14th
century, the City reached its climax of brilliancy.

In more recent years George Fox and John
Wesley preached in Carlisle; Archdeacon Paley was
Vicar of Stanwix, and Archbishop Tait, Dean of
Carlisle; Robert Burns spent a memorable evening
in the "Malt Shovel" inn; Sir Walter Scott was
married in the Abbey Church; and Charles
Dickens visited the City. Carlisle is described in
"Waverley," and the neighbouring country in
"Redgauntlet" and "Guy Mannering."

MERRIE CARLISLE.

Merrie Carlisle, Border City,
Valiant name in vivid ditty
　　Blithely sung of old:
Warden of a gallant story,
Rich in derring-do and glory,
　　Fare on ever bold.

Hill and fell, thy trusty warders,
O'er thine abbey, tower, bridge, borders,
　　Keep their watch afar:
Leal in dawn and noonday splendour,
Leal in hour of twilight tender,
　　And of midnight star.

Bright and broad thine Eden river
Winds mid holme and scaur for ever
　　By the castle hill;
Subtly with thine annals blending
Music, murmured in her wending
　　To the Solway still.

On his wedding day Sir Walter
Led his dear love to thine altar,
   Fair romantic town:
Lent his great name to thy story,
To the glamour and the glory
   Of thy long renown.

Mary, Queen of Scots, dwelt in thee:
Swift her captive eyes to win thee,
   Bright eyes dark with fate;
Edward, Cromwell, aye victorious,
Bonnie Charlie, nine months glorious,
   Galloped through thy gate.

Glint of helm and armour glancing
Eden saw, and chargers prancing
   In the tourney fight;
When stark reivers drave the cattle
Eden heard their stout spears rattle
   Northward through the night.

Eden heard, when morn was breaking,
Kinmont Willie's Warden waking
   Keen Scrope from his dream:
While the laughing rescuers follow
Bold Buccleuch swift as the swallow
   Skims o'er holme and stream.

Peel and castle on thy border,
Relics of an ancient order,
　　Frown forlorn to-day;
Valour casts its slough of rudeness,
Yet abides the soul of goodness
　　Though its forms decay.

Merrie Carlisle, Border City,
Valiant name in vivid ditty
　　Blithely sung of old:
Warden of a gallant story,
Rich in derring-do and glory,
　　Fare on ever bold.

CAREL CROSS

LAST MEETING OF ST. CUTHBERT AND ST. HERBERT AT CARLISLE, A.D. 685.

The Venerable Bede so loved the memory of St. Cuthbert that he persuaded the brothers of Lindisfarne to enrol his name among their own " in the white book of their holy congregation." Both in his " Ecclesiastical History " and his " Life of St. Cuthbert " he tells the exquisite story concerning the " venerable priest of the name of Herbert," who had " long been united to the man of God, Cuthbert, in the bond of spiritual friendship, and who, leading a solitary life in an island in the large marsh from which the Derwent rises, used to come to him every year and receive from him admonitions in the way of eternal life. When this man heard that Cuthbert was stopping in Carlisle, he came, according to his custom, desiring to be kindled up more and more by his wholesome exhortations in aspiring after heavenly things. When these two had drunk deeply of the cup of celestial wisdom, Cuthbert said, among other things, ' Remember, brother Herbert, that you ask me concerning whatever undertaking you may have in hand, and that you speak to me about it now, because after we shall have separated we shall see each other no more in this life. I am certain that the time of my death approaches.' Upon hearing these words Herbert threw himself at his feet with tears and lamentations, saying, ' I beseech you by the Lord not to leave me, but be mindful of your companion, and pray the Almighty Goodness that as we have served Him together on earth we may at the same time pass to heaven to see His light.' The Bishop (Cuthbert) applied himself to prayer, and having presently had intimation in spirit that he had obtained what he asked of the Lord, he said, ' Rise, brother, and do not weep, but rejoice, because the Heavenly Goodness has granted what we desired.' The event proved the truth of this promise and prophecy, for they never met again, but their souls departed from their bodies at one and the same moment of time, that is on the 20th March, and were joined together in a heavenly vision and translated at the same time by angels to the heavenly kingdom."

For eight years Cuthbert lived alone on a little island near Lindisfarne, in a hut open to the sky, whence he heard no voices but those of the winds, the waves, and the sea-mews. Herbert also dwelt in solitariness on his island in Derwentwater. The absolute isolation of the two anchorites makes their passionate friendship, with its inward depth and its presentiment of immortality, all the more touching. It shines like a star amid the darkness and tempest of the early middle-ages. The date of their meeting we may fix as June 685, and its place as " the Swifts," or holmes to the east of the bridge near Rickerby.

ST. CUTHBERT AND ST. HERBERT ON THE SWIFTS.

From his bird-haunted isle,
By many a moorland mile,
Came Cuthbert to Carlisle.

Lit by the June sunbeam
Blue glittered Eden stream,
Whereby he dreamt a dream:—

The Cymri sin forsook,
New names an angel took,
To write in Christ's white book.

He waked: Herbert was there;
For Cumbria, dear care,
Two hearts were knit in prayer.

They, to their Master's praise,
Through lustrous length of days
Were one in all His ways.

It was their wont to meet
Yearly; with eager feet
They came for counsel sweet:

Herbert from Derwent Lake,
Cuthbert, for his dear sake,
From Farne, where lone seas break.

Cuthbert spake, Brother dear,
I feel mine hour is near,
No more shall we meet here.

Soul of my soul thou art,
If aught be on thy heart
Speak now, for soon we part.

Leave me not, Herbert cried,
My father, brother, guide,
Like none on earth beside.

Yet, if it must be, pray
That on thy dying day
I too may go thy way.

Silence fell for a space,
Stone still was Eden's face
While Cuthbert sought this grace.

A skylark thrilled the air
Above the green holme where
The brothers knelt in prayer.

The skylark left the sky
And laid his music by;
Then Herbert sighed a sigh.

Rejoice, dear heart, rejoice,
Cried Cuthbert, for the voice
Whispers thou hast thy choice.

It shall be even so;
Know, brother, surely know
Thou goest when I go.

Christ praised they for this word,
Far in the spirit heard,
By home fore-feeling stirred.

They parted, and Bede saith,
When Cuthbert sank in death
Herbert breathed his last breath.

Was it on that same night
The brother saw a light
At Melrose, passing bright?

Two saints in shining state
Swift angels bore, elate,
Up to a golden gate.

Thence a great glory broke:
Trumpets in loud peal spoke;
Whereon the brother woke.

SOLWAY MOSS.

1542 A.D.

Between Gretna and Longtown the Solway Moss stretches northward to the Langholm hills. It is fringed with young birches. In November 1542, King James V (father of Mary, Queen of Scots) sent a large army from Caerlaverock to invade England. He gave orders that a herald should proclaim Oliver Sinclair, his favourite, generalissimo. This foolish proclamation enraged his proud nobles and turned his army into an agitated mob. Just then 300 English cavalry, under Dacre and Musgrave, advanced to reconnoitre. Seeing the Scots in confusion, they charged, scattered 10,000 Scottish troops, and took a thousand prisoners. The tidings fell like a thunderbolt on Caerlaverock. The king's heart was broken. In a few weeks he died, in the thirty-first year of his age. This crushing defeat exposed Scotland for years to a terrible spoliation and humiliation at the hands of King Henry VIII. In our Border annals there is not a more signal illustration of the weakness and madness of disunion than the disaster at the Solway Moss.

SOLWAY MOSS

November 1542, A.D.

Grow, birches, grow,
  Seed out to left and right:
Cover this Solway Moss
  Like a dead face from sight.

Spread, birches, spread,
  Spread quickly and afar:
O hide these bare peat hags
  From sun and moon and star.

This moor beheld
  Disunion poison power;
Down went a nation's pride
  In one chaotic hour.

Ten thousand broke
  Before three hundred men;
Harry, the Tudor King,
  Bled Scotland white again.

Rode from the field
A rider anguish-tossed,
To carry to his King
The tidings " all is lost."

Red sank the sun
In the November sea;
Redder a monarch's shame,
Caerlaverock, in thee.

Spread, birches, spread,
Spread quickly and afar:
O hide this Solway Moss
From sun and moon and star.

Carlisle Castle

Entrance Gateway and Keep

Sauceries and Stanwix

From Carlisle Castle

MARY, QUEEN OF SCOTS, AT THE SAUCERIES.

The "Sauceries" are the holmes between the Castle and the river. The name is derived from the willows (Salix, saugh) which once grew by the Eden and the Caldew.

After Langside, May 1568, Queen Mary crossed the Solway to Workington, and was conducted thence by Lowther to Carlisle. During her six weeks' stay in the Castle she was kept under strict, if kindly, surveillance by Lord Scrope and Sir Francis Knollys. In a letter to Queen Elizabeth she described her condition as so pitiable " not to say for a Queen but even for a simple gentlewoman " that she had no other dress than that in which she escaped from the field. A vast wardrobe was accordingly sent her, by the Regent Moray, from Holyrood. She was allowed to attend service in the Abbey, to walk on the Holmes and watch the game of football, and to ride out hunting the hare with her retinue. Ash trees were planted by Mary on the Queen's walk, but were cut down over a century ago, and a little later her rooms in the Castle were demolished.

It is strange to reflect that, although Mary Stuart at Carlisle was not yet twenty-six, she had been thrice wedded, the most brilliant figure in two courts, present at two battles waged in her behalf, an instrument in vast political designs, an accused criminal, an escaped captive. One is tempted to ask, what were the deeper thoughts concerning life of a personality so widely experienced, so variously gifted, and so evilly circumstanced. It is, perhaps, significant that after leaving Carlisle Mary appeared to be sympathetic to the Church of England, "received an English chaplain," and grew "to a good liking of the common prayer."

MARY, QUEEN OF SCOTS, AT THE SAUCERIES.

O river, sister river,
Changing, unchanging ever,
Fie, mud thy flow enfoldeth!
Nay, pardon sweet, it holdeth
Brave likeness of clean sky.
Prithee come tell me, river,
—Sooth to my heart deliver
When to thy bank I hie—
Our current, shall it never
Without mud mirror sky?
For ever and for ever,
Without a reason why,
Shall mud, dear heart, belie
Our kinship with clean sky?

O sweetheart, our spate changes
Scare away skyey things;
Joyance?—afar it ranges:
Love? fame?—have plaguey wings.
Nevertheless, O river,
A voice within me ever,
Albeit I know not why,
Whispers me and assureth
That what alone endureth,
Brave sister, is clean sky.
Yea, the calm voice assureth,
Albeit I know not why,
Alone at last endureth
Nor cloud, nor mud, but sky.

Prithee, come tell me, river,
What this same voice may be;
For ever and for ever
Thou flowest to the sea,
Thence doth some whisper carry
Tidings of heart that feels—
" Madam, we wait "—
           " Nay marry,
We hear how yon bell peals.
'Twas not our will to tarry.
Natheless, fair sir, we know
What duty thou dost owe.
Thanks for this timely call;
Attend him, maidens all."

O river, sister river,
Changing, unchanging ever,
Roll on, dear heart, roll on.
Pardon, I must be gone.
Thou wottest well, I ween,
I'm but a captive Queen.
Nevertheless, O river,
The voice within me ever,
Albeit I know not why,
Whispers me and assureth
Alone at last endureth
Nor cloud, nor mud, but sky.
Whence the calm voice? and why?
O sweetheart, by and by
The sea may make reply.

1

KINMONT WILLIE'S TOAST.

It is odd to find Kinmont Willie figuring as hero in ecclesiastical history—a moss-trooping Armstrong who robbed his neighbours of life as well as property. Archbishop Spottiswood devotes some sympathetic pages to the reiver, and the Scots Presbyterian ministers also took his side. For he had been taken by Salkeld of Corby, deputy for Lord Scrope the English Warden, in flagrant violation of border truce. The law of the marches was that the truce held till sunrise after the day of meeting, and Salkeld seized Kinmont as he was riding home to Morton-on-the-Sark on the evening of the truce at Kershope, in Liddesdale. After vain protests, Buccleuch, the Scots Warden, determined to pluck his man out of the lion's den, to wit the Castle of Carlisle, where Kinmont lay in irons, doomed to execution at Harraby. So with a band of young bloods, chiefly Scotts of his own clan, he crossed the Eden below Stanwix, just before the dawn of 13th April 1596, penetrated the Castle, and carried away Kinmont Willie, irons and all, without spilling a drop of English blood. Buccleuch's strategy was apparently this: With one half of the rescue party he stationed himself to the north of the castle wall, and filled the misty night with trumpet calls and shouts of command. Scrope and his officers rushed to that quarter and tried to estimate the numbers and formation of the Scots. Meanwhile the other half of Buccleuch's men stole round to the west wall, scaled it, ran to their comrade's prison, and carried him off. The postern by which they made their triumphant exit may still be seen.

They say that Red Rowan, "the starkest man in Teviotdale," carried Kinmont on his shoulders, with his irons or "spurs" still on, and Sir Walter Scott tells us that these were knocked off by the smith at a cottage near Longtown. Sir Walter also mentions that, some years later, when Queen Elizabeth demanded of Buccleuch "how he dared to undertake an enterprise so desperate and presumptuous?" the Scots Warden turned away her wrath by the bold answer, "Madam, what is it that a man dares not do?" "With 10,000 such men," said Elizabeth to a lord in waiting, "our brother of Scotland might shake the firmest throne in Europe."

The contemporary historians extol Buccleuch's exploit as the most daring deed of the age, and one enthusiast declares that the like of it "was never done since the memory of man, no not in Wallace dayis." It was the last achievement of Border chivalry. To us the glorious feature of the rescue is not simply its daring, but the spirit of comradeship it displays. Buccleuch stood by his man, who, on his part, was ready to render his chief any service. This personal interest, this human touch, this loyalty of man to man is worth remembering in the 20th century, when at times—though there is so much kindliness—everything seems to go by machinery, and the machines act like men and the men like machines, and apparently the only bond between men is the "cash nexus."

KINMONT WILLIE'S TOAST.

Up men, rise a',
Our toast is " Bold Buccleuch ";
For lads of mettle, leal and stark,
He does what man may do.
Drink deep, drink deep,
Let ilk man drain ilk cup,
Up, pledge Buccleuch wi' mug uplift,
Syne turn the beaker up.

Weel, weel, fause truce
Of a' things is maist vile;
While I rode hame they gruppit me
And jailed me in Carlisle.
Stone wa', stone wa',
And ne'er a blink o' hope:
Affhand ma weird was Hairribie
And twenty feet o' rope.

Salkeld, Salkeld,
Ilk man has his ain view,
But foul abuse o' Border truce—
How will that fit Buccleuch?
Keen Scrope, Keen Scrope,
His een fair sparked wi' glee,
"Kinmont," quo' he, "thy weird thou'lt dree,
Harraby comforts me."

"Lord Scrope, your rope
Frights not, nor can dismay
Marchmen," quo' I, "and by and by
Moonlight again we'll hae."
"Moonlight!" quo' he,
"Thief, wouldst thou mock at me?
Wi' moon and sun thou wilt be done,
Kinmont, on Harraby."

That nicht, that nicht,
Crowbars and axes banged;
I heard Red Rowan's voice sing oot
"Kinmont, thou'se no be hanged."
Rug-tug, rug-tug,
They tugged ma irons in vain,
Syne Rowan heaved me on his back
Gin I had been a wean.

"Sit free," quo' he,
"Saddle nor bridle ask,
Wow, but thae mighty spurs o' yours
Gie me an unco task."
Shoulders and neck
Like Rowan's ne'er hae been,
The starkest man in Teviotdale,
And toughest nag yet seen.

"Thanks, Scrope," cried I,
"For board and lodging free!
Gin ye should want the bill paid, Scrope,
In Scotland visit me.
Keen Scrope, Keen Scrope,
What o' the moonlight noo?
And wuddy tree on Hairribie?
Man, ye forgot Buccleuch."

Flashed red fire flame
Fra Carlisle beacon licht,
And syne the muckle auld town bell
Waked a' the bells wi' fricht.
Ding-dong, ding-dong,
Went keep and minster bells,
Clang, clang, ding-dong, ding-dong
Oot to the misty fells.

Bold, bold Buccleuch,
Gart blaw a bugle blast,
Syne wi' the lave to Eden ford
Red Rowan galloped fast.
Plash through the spate
We plunged to Stanwix brae,
Then skirled anither slogan blast
To blaw the wat away.

"Mount, lads, and ride,"
Spak up the bold Buccleuch,
"When I have said one parting word
To bid Lord Scrope adieu.
Warden," he cried,
"Be it by thee confessed,
We spilt no drop o' English blood
When harrying thy nest."

Wow, sic a ride!
Until the morning broke
Upon a sleepy blacksmith's cot;
The locn was soon awoke.
Crash gaed a spear
Close by the guidwife's head:
Oot tumbled smith, syne ceased to swear
And filed ma irons instead.

Doon fell the gyves.
Gin dawnin' wasna sweet?
I louped upon the dewy grass
To feel I owned my feet.
Free, hand and foot,
What can wi' that compare?
I mounted on a four-legged nag
Nor fashed Red Rowan mair.

Morton-on-Sark
Wi' its blue reek again,
The wife and bairns and dogs and a'
O gin they werena fain!
Good-bye, Carlisle!
Rescued by bold Buccleuch!
For men o' mettle, leal and stark,
He does what man may do.

Queen Bess, Queen Bess,
(Sic tidings quickly run)
Has speired Buccleuch how he daur do
The great deed he has done.
"Dare, madam, dare"
(To face her was nae fun)
"And what is there a man won't dare?"
Fair was the Queen's heart won.

"Hear him," quo' she,
Unto her chamberlain,
"Wi' good ten thousand men like him
We'd rule the earth and main."
Honour Buccleuch,
Who honours Scotland's name;
It smells sweet noo in ilka land,
—The rose o' knightly fame.

Up men, rise a',
Toast aince mair " Bold Buccleuch;"
For lads o' mettle, leal and stark,
He does what man may do.
Drink deep, drink deep,
Let ilk man drain ilk cup,
Up, pledge Buccleuch wi' mug uplift,
Syne turn the beaker up.

1

Fourteenth Century House, King's Arms Lane, Carlisle

GEORGE FOX AT CARLISLE.

In the 17th century in England the best men were to be found in gaol, and no man saw more of the inside of prisons than " the man in the leathern breeches "—George Fox, the Quaker. He was imprisoned in Nottingham, Derby, Launceston, London, Lancaster, Carlisle, Worcester, Scarborough, and other places, and only allowed to live as a free man during the last sixteen years of his life (1624—1690). At Carlisle, in 1653, after preaching in the Abbey, in the Castle, and at the Market Cross, with such effect that " many of the Baptists and the soldiers were convinced," and in a " steeple-house " where, under the word " the people trembled and shook and thought the steeple-house also shook," he was arrested by the magistrates and " committed to the prison as a blasphemer, heretic, and seducer !" The City confidently anticipated his execution, but a death sentence on such a charge was found to be illegal. Apparently it is uncertain where Fox was imprisoned. It would have gratified our sense of reverence for sacred places had the surmise proved correct which identified his gaol with the fourteenth century house in King's Arms Lane, which Dr. Bloxsome Day has kindly photographed for this book. But it seems more probable that Fox was confined either in the County gaol at the Citadel—if it was then in existence—or in the City gaol, which was over the Scotch

Gate, at the top of Rickergate Brow. From Fox's Journal we learn that one "musqueteer" was stationed at the door of his room, a second at the foot of the stair, and a third at the street door.   Later, Fox was sent down to the loathsome basement chamber or dungeon, " amongst the moss-troopers, thieves, and murderers."   Food was handed to him by his friends through the bars of the prison window, and " priests " came " to the grates to dispute."   One of his converts was a youth named James Parnel, who afterwards became a preacher and perished cruelly at Colchester. Bad as the Carlisle gaol was, " the prisoners," says Fox, " were all made very loving and subject to me, and some of them were convinced of the truth."   The gaolers, however, were extremely brutal, and it comforts one to learn that just before Fox was set at liberty, the Governor, accompanied by Anthony Pearson—" a justice of the peace in three counties," who " was convinced at Appleby by James Naylor and Francis Howgill, who were then prisoners there and brought before him "—came down to see the dungeon, expressed great indignation at its condition, and sent one of the two gaolers there to try it for himself.

It was natural that Fox—of all men—should describe the condition of men as that of " spirits in prison," who can only be set free by the voice of Him who carries the keys at His girdle, and has His witness in the human heart, by the inner light of the Spirit.

GEORGE FOX AND THE CARLISLE FRIENDS.
1653.

Kind friends, once in a dungeon
Below a castle stair,
I saw some strange wall scratches
And asked how these came there.

"Ah, once there was a captive,"
My gaoler friend replied,
"Who went mad in this dungeon,
Wrestling to win outside.

"With his poor frantic fingers
He made the marks you see,
Digging into the stone-work
In frenzy to be free.

"He dug and tore the stone-work,
Then gave as reason why,
'I'm boring through this hell-wall
To see the bright blue sky.'"

"Good gaoler friend, thy story,"
I said, "doth make me sad;
What are we all but captives
Who oftentimes go mad?

" Fain would poor souls in prison
    Escape their proper doom ;
They cannot quit their dungeon
    Save it be for their tomb.

" Only one Voice availeth
    To set the captive free :
Thank God, we hear it crying,
    ' Look, sinner, unto Me.'

" A waft of power still cometh
    With that Voice from on high :
Our dungeon roof disparteth,
    We see the open sky :

" Our dungeon doors fly open,
    We step outside again ;
And then our word wins entrance
    Into the hearts of men.

" But pity most poor captives
    To lust and pomp and pelf,
Stung with no noble frenzy
    To quit the cell of self."

Major Macdonald's Cell, Carlisle Castle

*The various devices shown were done by captive Officers of the
"Prince Charlie" rising*

MAJOR RANALD MACPHERSON
ON
THE DUKE OF CUMBERLAND.
AUGUST 1746. CARLISLE.

One of the haunting sights in the Castle is the work done on the walls between their cells by Major Macdonald, of Tyendrish, and gallant captive officers of the Prince Charlie rising. With sharpened nails or other instruments they carved the Percy and Dacre arms, the insignia of their regiments, the martyrdom of St. Sebastian, and various devices. To think of those brave fellows and their execrable doom makes one feel, with Waverley, as if one could never enter Carlisle again. Thirty-one executions, and skulls affixed to her gates, blotted hideously the chivalrous name of our Border City. After Culloden, such barbarous vengeance was inexcusable. The Duke of Cumberland, like Judge Jefferies, overdid his part. They dishonoured two noble vocations.

On Monday, 18th November 1745, Prince Charlie entered Carlisle in triumph and won favour by his gallant bearing and fair dealing. A month later he returned through the City close pressed by the Duke of Cumberland. The garrison of 400 men, which in an evil moment he left behind, were soon prisoners. On 16th April, 1746, Prince Charlie's enterprise was irretrievably ruined at Culloden; yet, months later, in August of that year, ninety-six Carlisle prisoners were sentenced to death, and thirty-one were actually murdered in cold blood, after a formal trial. Cumberland set £30,000 on his kinsman's head, but to their eternal honour not a single clansman would betray his prince.

MAJOR RANALD MACPHERSON,
Prisoner in Carlisle Castle,
under Sentence of Death, August 1746,
on
THE DUKE OF CUMBERLAND.

Some birds affront the sunshine,
Some fishes foul the seas,
Snakes desecrate the mountains
And plagues pollute the breeze :
   Be thy name named, O Cumberland,
   With noxious things like these.

Not red Culloden slakes thee,
Thy slogan is " kill, kill,
Let Highland blood make redder
Each heather moor and hill."
   Till crack of doom, O Cumberland,
   Be thy name " Butcher " still.

Thou settest store of money
Upon thy kinsman's head,
But who of all the clansmen
Will sell his Prince for bread?
   Thou hast thy lucre, Cumberland,
   They have white souls instead.

Highmore House, Carlisle, in 1745

*Occupied by "Bonnie Prince Charlie,"
and also by the Duke of Cumberland*

Thou canst not stain the honour
Of gallant captive foes,
Although thou doom their bodies
To feed foul carrion crows:
   A blot on her escutcheon
   To thy name Carlisle owes.

Brave seas encompass England,
Brave bens in Scotland stand,
No wave thy shame will cover,
No hill stream cleanse thy hand:
   Disowned is scarlet Cumberland
   By ocean and by land.

Some birds affront the sunshine,
Some fishes foul the seas,
Snakes desecrate the mountains
And plagues pollute the breeze:
   Be thy name named, O Cumberland,
   With noxious things like these.

THE BRAMPTON GIRL'S FEAR.

Brampton, an ancient town nine miles east north-east of Carlisle, figures in the two rebellions of the 18th century. In 1715 Mr. Foster took formal command of the Jacobite Army at Brampton, and proclaimed the Pretender king before the assembled crowd in the market place. The Jacobites were soon defeated at Preston.

In 1745 Prince Charles Stuart took up his quarters at Brampton in a house in High Cross Street. The Mayor and Corporation of Carlisle presented the keys of the City to Prince Charlie, on their knees, at Brampton. The following is an entry in the session records of the Presbyterian Church at Brampton for 1745:—" Novr. 10 and 17. No sermon. The Minister being out of town because ye Rebels were in it." The Presbyterians were loyal Hanoverians, but many others in the little town were partisans of the Stuart Prince.

When, after Culloden, six rebels were hanged in Brampton by order of Cumberland, the terror of all who had favoured Bonnie Prince Charlie may readily be imagined. This widely prevailing fear is the motive of the following little song.

"Bonnie Prince Charlie"

*From an original picture, the property of P. J. Canning Howard, Esq.,
Corby Castle, Cumberland*

THE BRAMPTON GIRL'S FEAR.

In our green lonnin', a' the lang day,
Kye hev been lowin', dowie and wae,
Eerily lowin' a' the day lang,
Sair it misgi'es me something is wrang.

It was at Lammas Jamie set sail,
How the wind whistled! Wow, sic a wail!
Sadly we parted, ne'er a word since;
And he loved Charlie, the Bonnie Prince.

In the owd ruin, aince was a kirk,
Sweetly we trysted, just before mirk,
Till through the window, ruined lang syne,
Stars keeked and tented his vow and mine:—

Aye to be faithfu', faithfu' till death,
Leal to each other to our last breath.
O but our heart filled! werena we fain?
Would I might clasp thee, Jamie, again.

Wakin' at midnight, lonesome I weep,
Were but my heart light, sound I should sleep;
Sadly we parted, ne'er a word since—
O hev they grupped him, true to his Prince?

In our green lonnin', a' the lang day,
Kye hev been lowin', dowie and wae,
Eerily lowin' a' the day lang,
Sair it misgi'es me, something is wrang.

THE THREE CROSSES OF THE SOLWAY.

The first of the three famous crosses within sight of the Solway is at Gosforth, in West Cumberland, and may be distinguished as the Saga Cross. It is not a Pagan but a Christian monument, of Irish workmanship, and dating probably from the 11th century. Yet the scenes portrayed are not from the Gospels, but from the Vala's prophecy concerning the "twilight of the gods," the final battle between the good gods of Valhalla and the powers of hell. According to Norse mythology, it is only at infinite cost that the reign of right is finally established. In an epoch-making paper, the late Rev. W. S. Calverley interpreted the Gosforth monolith as teaching that Christ, not Odin or Thor, Vidar or Balder, is Conqueror of Death and Hell, and Redeemer of the World. To minds steeped in Norse mythology the Gosforth cross spoke in a language they could understand, and drew parallels or showed contrasts between the heathen and the Christian faith.

The second cross stands in the Parish Church at Ruthwell, Dumfriesshire, and may be named the Runic Cross with the Saxon "Lay of the Holy Rood." Its date is generally assigned to the last decades of the 7th century. The Anglian workmanship is exquisite, and the scenes represented are mainly from

Bewcastle Cross (East Front)

the Gospels. But the special interest of the monument is that the Runic inscription is, beyond doubt, a quotation from an early English poem by Caedmon, or possibly by Cynewulf. The beautiful fancy of the rood, once a flourishing tree, describing the awful Burden it had to bear, and its sympathy with the sorrows of the Crucified, recalls the sorrow of nature for the death of Balder the Good, in the Norse mythology. Apparently in the 7th century, as in the 11th, the Christian missionaries or artists set the faith in relief against a background of pagan story.

The third cross is at Bewcastle, in North Cumberland, and is a memorial to Alcfrith, son of Oswy, and King of Deira. It has been called the noblest Christian monument on this side of the Alps, and its generally received date is 670 A.D. In his youth Alcfrith went over to Penda, the Pagan King of Mercia, and married Cyneburga, Penda's daughter. Later, he became zealously Christian, won to the faith Peada, Prince of Mercia—who was baptised in the Tyne, near the Roman wall—and with Oswy, defeated and slew Penda, at Winwaed, near Leeds, in 655 A.D. In the great Easter controversy, in 664, Oswy and Alcfrith took opposite sides. The sire, who had been educated at Iona, and spoke Gaelic, sympathised with the Columban missionaries; the son—intimate friend of Wilfrith—was a hot partisan of Rome. Their strife was bitter, and possibly the popular mind saw, in a fiery comet and a terrible plague of those days, a judgment of heaven upon a monarch who lived at war with his own father.

The vine-scroll on the Bewcastle memorial monument, and the knotwork symbol of the Trinity, are of unsurpassed English workmanship. But the western face is most significant. The upper panel represents S. John the Baptist and the Lamb; the middle panel the Risen Christ, with right hand uplifted in blessing, left hand holding a scroll, and feet treading down swine or dragons; and the lower panel a figure with bird on left wrist—probably St. John the Evangelist and his eagle, but possibly King Alcfrith and his hawk. Beneath the central panel are runes to this effect:—" Hwaetred, Wothgar, and Olfwolthu set up this lofty standard in memory of Alcfrith, late King and son of Oswy. Pray for (the high sin of?) his soul." Other names on the cross are Cyneburga, Cyneswitha, Ecgfrith, and Wulfhere. The monument proclaims " Christ, not Odin, is Lord of Light and Life, and Victor over evil." What is remarkable, those ancient crosses give no hint of the later adoration of the Virgin, and invocation of saints. They portray the Risen Christ as Himself the sum and substance of the Christian Evangel. Christendom may yet deem this simple early faith an ample creed.

Bewcastle Cross (West Front)

THE BEWCASTLE CROSS.
670 A.D.
HWAETRED
SPEAKS AT THE ERECTION OF THE MEMORIAL COLUMN
TO
ALCFRITH, KING OF DEIRA.
I.

Hwaetred, Wothgar, and Olfwolthu
Have hewn this slender shaft of stone
With English craft, and carved thereon
These sacred figures, signs, and runes,
In memory of Alcfrithu,
Once King, and son of Oswiu.
Eke that it be a standard proud,
In shape a lofty victor rood,
—Sign wherein Christians conquer foes,
As Oswald did at Heavenfield—
Whereto his folk may press with joy,
Strong in that faith which triumph won
And endless praise for Alcfrithu.
Battle he waged for the White Christ,
With sword of steel and sword of truth.
A nation to the faith he drew.
Lo, in the river, at the Wall,
Peada of Mercia was baptized
With all his nobles, thanes and thralls,
By Christ's grace, giv'n through Alcfrithu;
Who prayed that for his soul ye pray.

II.

Cyneburga was his Queen belov'd,
Daughter of Penda, Mercia's king.
Not their's was Penda's pagan creed;
Look on this rood and understand.
What Baldr could not be Christ was,
The Lamb of God, stainless and white,
Who wrought redemption for mankind.
Not Odin is the lord of light,
But Christ is Sun of Righteousness.
Not Igdrasil—the sun-god's horse,
Whose loud hooves through the welkin ring,
Its homeland, for it is but wind
Harnessed by Odin for a steed—
Is master of all things that breathe;
Giver and Lord of Life is Christ:
Whose emblem is not the rude Ash,
Wood of fierce javelin and spear,
But clusters of the peaceful Vine.
No maw of Hel-wolf shall devour
Earth, sky, and ev'n Valhalla's halls,
Sating itself with latest breath,
Of dying men and dying gods,
For Christ hath conquered Death and Hel.
Behold the Hel-wolves neath His feet.
Alcfrith waged war for the White Christ,
And prayed that for his soul ye pray.

III.

The sword of Alcfrith and his sire
Laid Penda and his hosts to sleep
At Winwaed, where the stream ran red
When Odin lowered his gold shield,
Letting his sons sink with the sun.
Thereafter between sire and son
Dark thoughts arose and war of words,
For Oswiu liked not that creed
Which learned Wilfrid taught Alcfrith
Concerning Roman Easter time.
Aidan he loved, Finan and Chad,
Colman too with his Culdee ways,
Eke that weird tongue Iona speaks.
And Alcfrithu abhorred the death
Of noble Oswin, king and saint,
Slain craftily by Oswiu;
Nor deemed the monastery built
By Oswy at Ingethlingum
Made fit atonement for foul crime.
Fell was the strife and rent the realm.
Alcfrithu and Deira frowned
On Oswy and Bernicia.
Northumbria trembled earthquake-riv'n.
Men's hearts were filled with bodeful fear.
Fierce flame streamed from the midnight sky.
Blue mid-day changed to cope of Hel,
Swart Hel, lampless and lightning-lit.
Wolves howled at noon and deemed it night.

Wherefore the dweller in his soul
Looked forth on Alcfrith fierily,
Most like that red and angry star
Which whitened faces through the land
Before the late black year of plague,
Foul as the Grendel of the fen.
Give heed that ye for Alcfrith pray,
For his sin, for his soul, and theirs
Whose names are graven on this Rood.

IV.

Alcfrith went hence ere Oswiu.
Dying, he asked that men should set
Within this border of the realm
A pillar tall of carven stone,
Shaped as a Rood, a banner proud
Whereon the folk might look with joy,
And none should worship pagan gods.
Eke that runes might be graved thereon,
Naming as one with him in faith
His brothers Ecgfrith, and Wulfhere,
Queen Cyneburg, Princess Cyneswitha,
Hwaetred, Wothgar, and Olfwolthu.
Thereafter, ere the silence fell,
He prayed ye for his soul should pray,
When far from forests he had fared
And fells, to king and hawk once dear.

Hexham Abbey

From an old print

THE BURNING OF THE HEXHAM BAIRNS.
(Red Ker o' Urr Haugh.)

We may date the last three centuries of Border
warfare from the ruthless sack of Berwick in 1296,
by Edward I. "Seventeen thousand persons," says
Tytler, "without distinction of age or sex, were
put to the sword, and for two days the city ran with
blood like a river." A more moderate estimate puts
the number slain at seven thousand. One incident
in particular burnt itself into the popular imagination. Thirty Flemish merchants, in the Red Hall,
held out to the last against the whole English Army.
Night came, and still it was not taken. Irritated by
this obstinate courage, the English set it on fire, and
buried its faithful defenders in the burning ruins.
The day was Good Friday. The Scots soon took
merciless revenge. An army, chiefly of Galloway
men, under the Earls of Ross, Menteith, and Athole,
made an inroad on England and ravaged Redesdale
and Tynedale. At Hexham they burnt the monastery,
and shutting a number of song school children in a
hall, set it on fire in revenge for the burning of the
Flemish merchants. The following lines impute the
instigation of this terrible deed to a Galloway Scot,

Red Ker of Branded Lea, near the Haugh of Urr, and suggest that, even in that ferocious age, the general conscience felt that so inhuman a crime against childhood must be overtaken by retribution. This incident would be too grim to recall, did it not illustrate the folly of human vengeance, and the tendency of one merciless deed to give birth to another. If there be any warrant in nature for such poetic justice as was meted out to Red Ker, it is certainly a benignant provision that the race of the cruel is short-lived.

RED KER O' URR HAUGH.

Do ye mind yon tree on Branded Lea,
Red Ker o' Urr Haugh,
Yon oak sae weird it maks ye feared?
By the big stane it stands alane,
White, withered, blasted bare as bane,
Red Ker o' Urr Haugh.

Ilk bird ye see aye shuns yon tree,
Red Ker o' Urr Haugh;
They winna sing on a cursèd thing.
The lightning struck where strong it stood,
The lightning withered up its blood;
Blasted, it kens the fear o' hell,
And, ghost-like, shivers at itsel',
Red Ker o' Urr Haugh.

Do ye mind yon work near Hexham Kirk,
Red Ker o' Urr Haugh,
Between the gloamin' and the mirk?
The Sang Schule bairns were in their ha';
Wha roared, "Up, Scots, and fire them a',
Mind Holy Friday and burn awa'"?
Red Ker o' Urr Haugh.

Oftwhiles ye see yon cursèd tree,
Red Ker o' Urr Haugh,
Yon oak sae weird it maks ye feared!
Nae birdie sings there shade nor shine;
Nor bairn will sing o' Red Ker's line;
Ilk bonnie wee thing ye maun tine.
The lightning struck where strong it stood,
The lightning whiles dries up the blood;
Blasted, it kens the fear o' hell,
And, ghost-like, shivers at itsel',
Red Ker o' Urr Haugh.

LINDSEY'S LAMENT.

Haughton Castle, on the North Tyne, once a
home of the Widdringtons, is a 14th century
tower house. Like most old castles it has its legend.
In the reign of Henry VIII, Haughton's men
captured by night Archie Armstrong, a Border freebooter, brought him at sunrise to Haughton, and
immured him in the castle dungeon. Early next
morning, Haughton rode off to York to meet Cardinal
Wolsey, taking the dungeon keys with him. On his
return, he was horrified to find that Armstrong had
been starved to death. Thereafter, the reiver's wraith
haunted the Castle.

Regarding an expression in Lindsey's curse, I
seem to have read somewhere that a curse was always
effectual if spoken in time; if, for instance, it were
pronounced on a murderer before the blood of his
victim had dried on his finger nails, or the red hand
had been cleansed.

LINDSEY'S LAMENT.

O Tyne rins slow and drumlie
  Below the castle wa';
They've starvit Archie Armstrong,
  The bravest o' them a'.

They couldna' tak' him waukin',
  They grupped him in his sleep,
Syne brocht him ower at sunrise
  In chains to Haughton keep.

He trysted me for Friday
  Beneath the capon tree;
O never more will Archie
  Keep gloamin' tryst wi' me.

Birds sing within the greenwood,
  Lambs skip upon the lea;
I gave my troth to Archie,
  O gin I could but dee.

They locked him in their dungeon
  Below the castle stair,
Woe's me, it was a Friday
  When Archie starvit there.

He cried in vain for water,
  In vain he cried for bread,
He wrastled sair wi' hunger,
  On Friday he lay deid.

Lang syne ma minnie said it,
  O why did I forget?
" Ne'er mak a tryst for Friday,
  It never prospered yet."

Black fa' the curse on Haughton,
  O let it soon begin,
Black fa' the curse on Haughton
  And sink his soul for sin.

Let aye a wraith ilk midnight
  Fricht Haughton's een frae sleep,
Let aye a wraith at midnight
  Scare Haughton in his keep.

They say he didna mean it,
  And gie his knaves the blame,
Wha left the reiver foodless
  When Haughton was fra hame.

I never will believe it;
  O let the curse begin,
Black fa' the curse ilk midnight
  On Haughton and his kin.

I've put the curse upon him,
  The curse that never fails;
I spak it ere the blood dried
  Upon the finger nails.

O what's wrang wi' the sunshine,
  That I'm sae sick o' life?
O what's wrang wi' the skylark,
  It stabs me like a knife?

O what can ail the dawnin'
  Was aince so fresh and sweet?
And what can ail the gloamin'?
  O gin I could but greet.

Ma heart's like stane within me,
  I never loved but ane;
I'm done wi' love and likin';
  I canna love again.

O for the tryst on Friday
  Beneath the capon tree;
I gave my troth to Archie,
  And canna thole nor dee.

O Tyne rins slow and drumlie,
  Below the Castle wa',
Wae's me for Archie Armstrong,
  The brawest o' them a'.

BATTLE MARCH OF THE COVENANTERS.

The Covenanters were mainly West Country peasants and farmers, goaded into rebellion by religious oppression on the part of the State. When men like Brown of Priesthill were shot at their farm door, and young women like Margaret Wilson were drowned in the Solway, the Covenanters felt that there was nothing for it but to fight and die. Their cause, like the grass, would but grow the thicker the oftener it was mown down. The language of the Covenanters is coloured by the graphic imagery of the Old Testament. They dreamt of a time when Scotland would exult in freedom, like " a hind let loose," satirised their opponents, content with civil and religious tyranny, as " Issachar," the " ass couching between his two burdens," and lauded the faithful as " Naphtali " the valiant " wrestler " for right. There is, I believe, a tradition that they marched into battle singing the twenty-third psalm to a tune which repeats the last two lines of each stanza, and has in it the shrill note of pipes and the roll of drums.

Regarding the Covenanters, Robert Burns, as in most matters, speaks from the heart of the Scottish people : —

"The Solemn League and Covenant
    Now brings a smile—now brings a tear;
But sacred freedom, too, was theirs,
    If thou'rt a slave, indulge thy sneer."

BATTLE MARCH OF THE COVENANTERS.

Lift high our Covenanting flag
  In face of all our foes;
Their gain is loss, and our loss gain,
  The mown grass thicker grows:
    Their gain is loss, and our loss gain,
    The mown grass thicker grows.

Our saints were drowned in Wigtown Bay;
  They live for evermore,
On after time their praise will break,
  As waves break on the shore:
    On after time their praise will break,
    As waves break on the shore.

On moor and hill His martyrs fall,
  Whose blood cries from the clod;
Their bright souls reign with saints on high,
  And shine as stars of God:
    Their bright souls reign with saints on high,
    And shine as stars of God.

They shine on glen and hill of home,
  They shine on shore and sea,
And with the sons of morning sing
  The new song of the free:
    And with the sons of morning sing
    The new song of the free.

Upon high places of the field
  Let us do valiantly,
Till Scotland, like a hind let loose,
  Exults in liberty:
    Till Scotland, like a hind let loose,
    Exults in liberty.

Couching beneath his burdens twain,
  Let Issachar lie low!
But in God's Name will Naphtali
  Still wrestle with the foe:
    But in God's Name will Naphtali
    Still wrestle with the foe.

The lion slinks back to his den,
  The leopard to his hill,
Before the fire of God that burns,
  To ward His people still:
    Before the fire of God that burns,
    To ward His people still.

From tyrant force, and craft of hell,
  And maw of beast of prey,
His glorious arm His flock shall fend,
  Harried in Galloway:
    His glorious arm His flock shall fend,
    Harried in Galloway.

(All reverently unbonneting.)

Yea, though I walk in death's dark vale,
  Yet will I fear none ill;
For thou art with me, and Thy rod
  And staff me comfort still:
    For thou art with me, and Thy rod
    And staff me comfort still.

THE DERWENTWATER LIGHTS.

The young Earl of Derwentwater owned estates at Keswick, but Dilston Castle in Northumberland was his favourite home. He was exceedingly beloved by his tenants and neighbours. In the Jacobite Rebellion of 1715, which ended disastrously at Preston, Derwentwater was the most heroic leader. He was executed at Tower Hill, 24th February 1716. That night, it is said, there was a brilliant display of aurora borealis, and the northern streamers are still known on Tyneside as "the Derwentwater lights." Educated in France, the young Earl married a French lady, and at Keswick she was bitterly blamed for instigating him to rebel, bidding him, when he hesitated, exchange his sword for her fan. So keen was the feeling that the young widow was forced to withdraw from Keswick to Dilston Castle, on the Tyne, where she was more kindly received. According to tradition, the mind of the unfortunate lady became unhinged, and sometimes at night she might be seen standing on Dilston Tower with lighted torch, or wandering through the grounds, as if seeking for her dead lord.

THE DERWENTWATER LIGHTS.

FEBRUARY 24TH 1716.

Strange lights in the February sky!
    Friend, what can it mean?
Glimmering over old Dilston Tower,
    Strange lights yestreen.

Dule, dule within Dilston Tower,
    What tears there will be!
O Derwentwater, our loving Earl,
    Clay-cold lies he.

Gold-bright were his sunny locks,
    Blue, blue were his een,
Kindlier smile and a kindlier hand
    Never were seen.

Larks over the London Tower
    Sang sweet in the sun;
O Derwentwater, how sweet their song
    When thine was done.

Will never a bonny bird
    Sing what he would say?
Sing a kind word to his lady dear
    In dule and wae.

Lone robin upon her sill
  Pecks aye at the pane;
This is the owercome o' his song—
  " Never again."

O never will lark and merle,
  Nor bird o' the spring,
Waken the ear o' her sleeping Earl
  To hear them sing.

Strange lights in the February sky!
  What tale do they tell?
Angels are signalling Dilston Tower
  " All's well, all's well."

All's well wi' the bonny Earl;
  Woe's me for his queen,
Wringing her hands for his voice, his smile,
  And glancing een.

Dule, dule, up in Dilston Tower,
  Black sorrow and dule;
Black it will be in the summer time,
  Blacker at Yule.

White, white upon Dilston Tower,
  Torch light in her hand,
Seeking her lord in the mirk midnight,
  Ghost-like she'll stand.

Lone, gliding round Dilston Tower,
  Looks she for her mate,
Seeking him still in each bower and glade,
  And at each gate.

Salt tears by the Derwent Lake,
  Soft tears by the Tyne;
Gentle and simple on hill and dale
  Mourn Radcliffe's line.

Strange lights in the February sky!
  Friend, what can it mean?
All bright up yonder, but deid mirk here:
  Strange lights yestreen.

THE GILSLAND QUESTION.

In " Guy Mannering " Sir Walter Scott describes
with zest the wild moorland and mountain country
about Bewcastle and Gilsland. It was at Gilsland,
with its Spa and Mumps Ha', its popping stone and
lovely wooded glen of the Irthing, that, in his twenty-
seventh year, he met the lady who afterwards became
his wife. Gilsland sets Scott before the imagination
in the ever attractive character of a youthful wooer;
and one wonders how so great an artist and so gallant
a man put the question, the answer to which—" Yes "
or " No "—is so fateful to an ardent lover. Gilsland
tradition, greatly daring, asserts that at its own
" popping stone " Scott's question received a happy
answer from Miss Carpenter, whom he afterwards
married at the Abbey Church of Carlisle.

THE GILSLAND QUESTION.

" No " is a sky of winter
   Freezing a midnight sea;
" Yes " is a burst of summer
   And the blue waves' glinting glee;
Is it winter and midnight, maiden,
   Or summer and noon for me?

Silent awhile is the maiden
   Beside the Gilsland stone;
Then her eyes shine love-laden,
   " Yes " is the choice they own.
So it was noon and summer,
   Unchanging with the sun,
For hearts that heard the music
   Waking when love was won.

The Popping Stone, Gilsland

Where Sir Walter Scott proposed to Miss Carpenter,
whom he afterwards married

QUENDRIDA, PRINCESS OF MERCIA.
819 A.D.

At Clent, in Worcestershire, in the 9th century,
a chapel was erected to St. Kenelm the boy King
of Mercia, youngest and most pathetic of British
saints, who at the age of seven was murdered by the
craft of Princess Quendrida, his sister, that her lover
might come to the throne. Toward the end of the
18th century, some workmen, while excavating
the ruined monastery of Winchcomb, in which,
according to the monkish chronicles, the body of
the boy-king had been buried beside that of his
father, lighted on a little stone coffin beside a larger
one, under the eastern window of the Church. They
raised the lid. Within were a little dust, fragments
of bone and skull, and a long-bladed knife, which fell
in pieces in the attempt to remove it.

The monkish version of the story is that a white
dove deposited on the altar of St. Peter's at Rome
a scroll on which was inscribed a Saxon couplet :—

In Clent, in Caubage, Kenelm, King-borne,
Lyeth under a thorne, his head off-shorne.

The Pope ordered the Mercian ecclesiastics to make
diligent search for the body of the slain prince,
and priests, monks, and canons, with the Bishop of
Mercia at their head, proceeded forthwith in long
procession to the forest.   There they found a cow
lowing pitifully beside what seemed a newly-laid
sod.   The earth was removed, the body of the prince
discovered, the bells of the neighbouring churches
straightway began " to rongen a peale without
manne's help," and a beautiful spring of water burst
out of the excavated hollow.   For many centuries
St. Kenelm's Well was a resort of pilgrims, and an
annual fair was held there till the year 1784.   Bird
and beast, tree and spring, conspired with man to
bring the hidden crime to light, as if nature were
alert, aware, and resolute, and the soul of things
were moral.   It is a beautiful mediæval gloss on the
text: " Be sure your sin will find you out."

QUENDRIDA, PRINCESS OF MERCIA.
819 A.D.

Quendrida, in the mead of kine
The cow lows: read to me the sign.

What ails thee, mother, at the mead?
A cow lows: what is there to read?

Within the mead there grows a thorn,
The white cow lows there night and morn.

What ails thee, mother, at the tree?
Fresh is its bloom and fair to see.

The white thorn shadeth burial sod:
The white cow crieth there to God.

When cattle low with doleful sound
Doth some one's blood cry from the ground?

Quendrida, beasts cry not in vain.
Doth Kenelm live, or is he slain?

I sent the boy to hunt the deer
And armed him with his bow and spear—

Woe's me, O woful hunting day,
My son, thy brother, was the prey.

Who profits if the child be dead,
Wilt thou not rule in Kenelm's stead?

O would thy sire were with us still,
Then had thy Wulfhere wrought no ill
Against our house: nor had his knife
Cropped the sweet bud of Kenelm's life.

In Kenelm's blood, to be a King,
Would Wulfhere dip my bridal ring?

What found they underneath the thorn?
Thy brother's head, who was king-born:
His head, his body, and a knife—
Wulfhere's, who taketh thee to wife:
These things found in the mead of kine
Prove Wolfhere's guilt, and likewise thine.
    Hearken, Quendrida, to that bell,
    What tale doth its slow tolling tell?

Who knoweth what the church bells toll?
If Kenelm's dead, God rest his soul.

Name not that Name; he sleepeth well.
Quendrida wakes to fire of hell.
Yea, kind earth's gifts henceforth unite
To hold thy guilt before thy sight.
Hereafter shall thy haunted mind
Hear his voice wail in every wind:
Hereafter every living well
Shall of thy dark crime's foulness tell:
Hereafter shall the thorn in flower
Confront thee with thy judgment hour:
Hereafter, when the cattle low,
Thy conscience shall sweet hope forgo:
Hereafter, when the church bells toll,
Thou shalt bewail thy death-doomed soul:
Lost, lost for ever, ever lost,
From pang to pang of torment tossed—
   Toll, bell, toll o'er the mead of kine
   And let Quendrida read the sign.

Town Hall, Carlisle, in 1745

POEMS

OF THE

CHRISTIAN TRADITION.

THE PROPRIETOR.

THE WORLD IS YOURS.

A reach of broad river,
White sailing whereon
A cygnet and swan;
Upon the green holme
Lambs frolic and roam;
High up in the blue,
Sun-hidden from view,
A lark carols clear
" Joy, Easter is here."
This heard I and saw
And blessed the good Giver;
Indefeasible law
Lets me own it for ever.
The heavens and the earth
Are yours from your birth.
From that mighty whole
Take into your soul
As much as you can
Of beauty and joy,
To greaten life's span
As man and as boy.
Be sure that the Maker
Loves a brave taker;
That—seers declare—
Is why nature is there.
What! if by a guest
It must be confessed
To his Host at the last
He has spurned His repast,
Shall so brutish a clod
Be well pleasing to God?
Soul, be thou a taker,
Not a churl to thy Maker.

THE OLD AGE PENSIONER.

ENDURE HARDNESS.

Hard hit, he did not fate indict;
Deeming that life is ordered right
By One Whose plan is infinite,
He hoped, and hid his hurt from sight:
Like that true-tempered Border knight,
Borne down at sunset in the fight,
Who lay still in the cold moonlight
And bled into his armour bright.

CHARITY.

YONDER IS THE SEA, GREAT AND WIDE.

Ribs of a wreck from a far bank of sand
Scowl at the shore, when the water is low;
School urchins wade through the wide pools and
    stand
Perched on the grim wreck, and waving their hand
Beckoning playmates too timid to go.

In sweeps the tide: the lads scramble and plash,
Eager the sheltering seabeach to win;
On come the rollers with thundering crash,
Hiding the wreck 'neath their gallop and dash,
Covered as charity covers a sin.

THE DEATH OF A POET.

THE CREATION ITSELF ALSO SHALL BE DELIVERED.

Calm as the mountain was the loch;
Blue sky was mirrored in the water
As deeply as a father's mind
Within the being of his daughter.
High vision held the noontide hour;
A skylark, soaring from the heather,
By song revealed what birch and pine,
Moor, loch, and mountain saw together.

Warm odours from the breath of June
Stole wooingly upon the senses;
Blithe brooklets tinkled elfin peals
To joy, in all its moods and tenses;
Sudden a shade and tremor fell,
The rosy cheek of joy was paling
With shoot and pang of chilling fear;
Above the loch a hawk was sailing.

Appalled, moor, loch, and mountain saw
Dark death slow in the welkin wheeling,
To strike their soaring poet down;
Their lorn heart thrilled with fellow-feeling.
Kind nature, subject to decay,
On tiptoe stands the day awaiting
When social fellowship shall be
Secure from death disintegrating.

THE REIGN OF MAN.

THOU HAST PUT ALL THINGS UNDER HIS FEET.

I

God of the sun, the stars, the wind,
  The mountains and the sea,
.What end was present to Thy mind
  When Thy hand fashioned me?

I do not, like Thy stars and sun,
  A punctual course fulfil,
Nor, as Thy winds and waters, run
  Swift-paced to do Thy will.

A sentinel I do not keep
  The watch appointed men,
As, leal in waking and in sleep,
  Thy mountains ward a glen.

Well may Thy steadfast heaven smile,
  And earth and sea be glad,
But rebel man, rebuked meanwhile,
  Is by their joy left sad:

Sad as a ruined temple, lone
  'Mid desolate sand dunes,
Or relic of lorn standing-stone,
  With wind-eroded runes.

In man some restive impulse mars
  Creation's loyal psalm;
I know, at least, my unrest jars
  With her eternal calm.

Profanely hath my perverse heart
  A rebel flag unfurled;
And yet, still perverse, I am part
  Of Thy vast ordered world.

God of the sun, the stars, the wind,
  The mountains and the sea,
What end was present to Thy mind
  When Thy hand fashioned me?

II

Lo, as a whisper from some star,
  In answer to my cry,
A calm voice reached me from afar
  And silenced all reply.

" Thy trembling harp He gladlier hears,
  Since thou can'st disobey,
Than all the music of the spheres
  Which cannot choose but play.

" In man, her lord, doth nature own
  Her hope: nor is it vain;
In Christ man risen to his throne
  Reigns, and shall ever reign.

" In Him ev'n now in kingly state
   Man rules yon world and this:
The open secret of his fate
   No wakeful ear can miss.

" A hearing ear still gives to man
   An understanding soul;
Love speaks: if heard, her whispers can
   Cast bright beams on the goal.

" Will thou to hear: He is not dumb;
   Vision attends His voice;
What men contemplate they become,
   Be life or death their choice.

" Only adore thou and be still:
   The desert shrub shall flame
With fire of dawn, and sky and hill
   Kindle beneath the same.

" In all things shall thy quickened sight
   A look of promise see;
The world in resurrection light
   Is big with things to be.

" And life, like that Red Sea of old
   Smitten by Moses' rod,
Opens to let the way unfold.
   Thine end?   Man's reign in God."

BEETHOVEN'S PORTRAIT.

SHE BRAKE THE CRUSE.

I

Here frowns a demigod
Strong with the strength of hills,
Fierce with the rage of seas,
Sad with the sadness of life;
Yet with benignant hand
Bringing to mortal men
Gift of Promethean fire,
Flame of a quenchless hope.

II

Lord of the realm of sound,
Trod he the world of men,
Exile from some fair star
Where is no speech but song.
Stricken by cruel fate,
Deaf to dear sounds of earth,
Prisoned within himself;
Yet in God's gentleness
Heard he as no man heard
Strains of the melody
Sung by bright sons of God
Over a world new-born.

III

Lo, at the touch of his art
—Sounding deep places within,
Gifting the spirit with wings—
Grow we new men to ourselves;
Pass the strait limits of sense,
Stir with a tumult of hopes
Exultantly sure of their crown;
Catch the far gleam of a world,
Richer, diviner than this;
Thrill at the moan of the sea
Sundering us from its shore,
Black sea of sorrow and doubt,
Loneliness, evil and death,
Booming in bass at our feet;
Soar again, envisaging
Bright arcs of rainbow and sky,
Joyfully soar as we hear,
Far on celestial heights,
Pealing of numerous bells
Chiming with voices afar
In the dear city of God.

IV

Feel we such awe at his name,
As when we suddenly sail
Into a sunset at sea,
Passionate, mystic, sublime;
Splendour of colour and form
Silencing voices of men;
Symbol of glorious life
Radiant, holy, divine,
Passing earth's power to endure;
Sacrament spread in the heavens,
Silently sealing this faith:—
Infinitude is our home,
Wherefore th' elect of mankind
Lift up their brow to the skies,
Kindle with rapture of hope,
March to the music of God;
Lavishly pour out their soul,
Breaking the costliest cruse,
Shedding through every room
And on the highway without
Odour and sweetness of nard;
Feel, that their brothers may feel,
See, that their brothers may see,
Hear, that their brothers may hear.

THE COUNCILLOR.

WHAT SHALL A MAN BE PROFITED?

Eager, self-confident, aware,
He looks efficient and all there,
    The Councillor:
A man of business with an air
Of having little time to spare.

He does not quickly trust, nor deems
That any man is what he seems,
    The Councillor:
He knows all is not gold that gleams;
He sees the motes in the sunbeams.

Blandly he says—when bluntly told,
By broken men, his soul is sold,
    The Councillor—
" Men must by any means make gold
Would they not be left in the cold.

" Although we may not quite agree
As to just trade, take it from me,
    The Councillor,
As solid truth and plain to see,
All trade answers the golden key.

"Business is business, that says all,
Whether the fact hit you or gall
   The Councillor:
When strong men hold the market, small
Traders must needs go to the wall."

When civic parties are at strife
He is a power in public life,
   The Councillor:
Demonstrating that it is rife
With ills that need *his* pruning knife.

A stout friend of the poor, 'tis true,
While the main burden falls on you,
   The Councillor:
But touch himself, he shifts his view
And pleads that theft will never do.

Although a man well on in years,
He is not wedded like his peers,
   The Councillor:
At lives of twain made one he jeers,
"Which one?" he says, is what he fears.

A winged word flies abroad one day,
"Our old friend has not long to stay,
   The Councillor:
A fatal seizure, so they say."
"No hope then?" "Not a single ray."

He passed away and left undone
Rich enterprises just begun.
    Poor Councillor!
Men asked then what *he* lost or won
Whose work had ceased beneath the sun.

" He did not take bad luck with grace,"
  Some whispered, " but with angry face,
    The Councillor:
As Swift's rat made a fierce grimace
When dying in a poisoned place."

Others replied, " Let dead men's faults
Be buried with them in their vaults.
    Poor Councillor!
Whose life is free from base assaults
By knaves whose own life badly halts?

" Of sorners there is never dearth;
  He made and paid his way on earth,
    The Councillor:
A thrifty nature from his birth;
Know ye not what our friend died worth?"

" Of hearts that loved him do ye wist?"
  Asked others: " Is he really missed,
    The Councillor?
Or set ye his name in their list
Whose soul the golden idol kissed?"

From unkind judgment most men shrink;
A lowered coffin makes them think.
    Poor Councillor!
Yet some aver, with nod and wink,
His gave a queer metallic clink.

Into the Higher School has passed,
By his own choice and liking classed,
    The Councillor.
What men should let go, what hold fast,
What microscopic deem, what vast,
What true life means he knows at last.

WELCOME TO THE LATEST ARRIVAL.

WHERE THERE IS NO VISION THE PEOPLE PERISH.

Welcome, welcome to our planet,
   Darling child,
Starry heavens overspan it,
God gave it to men to man it.

Though our wide domain be vaster,
   Gallant boy,
Than our cloudy mind can master,
Mind is clearing fast and faster.

Lest the good as best thou ratest,
   Child of earth,
Know of all things love is greatest,
And its best gifts are its latest.

That we may win to our haven,
   Sailor bold,
Storms are sent us to be brave in.
Perils only daunt the craven.

For the end of all our testing,
   Scholar bright,
Is to make us rich, investing
In the truest, fairest, best thing.

When we reach our destination,
    Heaven-born,
We shall know the high vocation
Set before each man and nation.

Only one thing on our planet,
    Gallant boy,
Is so base that, when we scan it,
Plain it is that men must ban it.

'Tis suspicion of our mission,
    Heaven-born;
Faith is ever life's condition,
Lack of vision is perdition.

Life, with springs in God, thou sharest,
    Darling child,
When to love and serve thou darest
Then the crown of life thou wearest.

MOTHER AND SON.

AS ONE WHOM HIS MOTHER COMFORTETH.

In Paradise, beneath the trees
  Where leaves of healing grow,
She weaves a coronal of these:
  And rests from care and woe:
Then softly sings, " Time, speed away,
Bring him, dear Time, to endless day."

The waters listen while she sings,
  Wherein, to mother eyes,
Remembered, far off, former things
  Are mirrored heavenly-wise:
Louder she sings, " Time, speed away,
O bring him soon to endless day."

A glory brightens, saints surround
  The mother by the stream:
With song the blessed fields resound,
  While Splendours glance and gleam,
Soft singing, " Time, speed fast away,
Bring him, dear Time, to endless day."

"Rejoice, rejoice," a trumpet peals,
　"He is at hand, rejoice."
New warmth within her heart reveals
　His presence, while his voice
Whispers, "O mother, far away
I heard thee call and could not stay.

"In lonely visions of the night,
　A breath from far-off skies
Rent the thin film that hides from sight
　The infinite surprise:
I heard thee calling, 'Come away,'
　And came to thee and endless day."

FATHER AND DAUGHTER.

I THOUGHT AS A CHILD.

"Why do you say the sunshine,
  Father, is bright to-day?"
A little maid makes sunshine,
  Or drives it clean away.

She frowns—the dark clouds gather
  And heavy is the air:
She smiles—the black clouds scatter
  And all is fresh and fair.

"Is that the secret, father,
  You told me I should know:
The way to make fine weather
  Come, and bad weather go?

"I think you mean our temper
  Makes things look dark or bright:
If good—why there is sunshine,
  If bad—why it is night."

You've read my riddle, dearie,
  Winning the promised prize:
Yet only eight blue summers
  Shine in your two blue eyes.

TRIPTYCH OF CHILDHOOD.

OF SUCH IS THE KINGDOM.

I.

Question.

Whence, little one, whence
Art thou come here?
Did some white ray pass
O'er the sea of glass
And disappear,
To gleam out on earth
Through the gates of birth
As the infant grace
Of thy sweet face:
Caught in the soft mesh
Of fading flesh
For many a year
Of time and space?

II.

Song.

As a bird within the nest
Safe beneath its mother's breast
Gently cared for goes to rest,
Sleep, little one, sleep.

God gives His belovèd sleep.
Dream, and smile, and slumber deep,
While their watch His angels keep:
Sleep, little one, sleep.

His own Son was once a child,
Holy, harmless, undefiled,
And He slept and dreamt and smiled:
Sleep, little one, sleep.

He whom saints and angels praise,
Who the Ancient is of Days,
Recollects the children's ways:
Sleep, little one, sleep.

III.

Hope.

How mystical is childhood's sleep!
  But must we never know
The mystery and meaning deep
  Of those years long ago,

When fancies fresh as morning dew
  Fell from the open sky,
And visions hid from manhood's view
  Brightened the childish eye:

When of life's load of heavy care
  And wintry weight of woe,
The soul was all as unaware
  As daisies are of snow?

Perchance when our brief day is o'er
  And we have passed the bourne,
Once more upon the farther shore
  Our childhood may return:

And from far years long wrapped in night
  The morning tide arise,
Dawning on our enraptured sight
  All wonder and surprise.

THE PHILOSOPHER'S DREAM.

Alles ist ich.

ALL IS VANITY.

All in the depths of darkness drear
  Where no light ever is,
And unclothed spirits far and near
  People the vast abyss,
A dreamer writhed and wrestled sore
  Upon his bed of night,
Hearing about him surge and roar
  The nether infinite.

Within him all his past awoke
  Like mist out of a sea,
To wrap him in its clammy smoke
  And cold obscurity.
Anon his record glared and broke
  As if in flames of ire,
While lightning gleams of thought provoke
  The self-consuming fire.

On any hand
No rest found he;
Nor in that land,
Of outlawry
From realms of peace
Shone there one ray
Hope of a day
His pain should cease.

He turned aye
And spurned aye
His book of days bygone,
Unresting
While testing
Its pages everyone.
At last
He passed
To philosophic calm,
Pain lulling and dulling
With transcendental psalm.

What is it all but a dream—the manifold world
  we see—
Woven of sights and of sounds only appearing to be?

Naught but the mind exists: it moveth ever anew
On through its forms of thought, nor is an end
  in view.

Time and space, cause and effect, beauty and duty
  and God—
Lured on by spectral guides, mind treadeth the way
  it hath trod.

Round and round on itself turneth the wheel of the
  soul,
Grinding phantasmal grain by forces beyond its
  control.

Universe? Nay but myself, only myself, do I see:
Phases and shiftings and modes alone of an infinite
  me.

Into the circle of self, whose limit nowhere appears,
Shut is the vastness of space and fulness of all the
  years.

Out of the circle of self may we endeavour to fly
When by a dead lift, men can raise themselves up
  to the sky.

Blessed ones rest in God, related alone to the true,
Free and at peace in a realm where He makes all
  things new.

Prisoned are we in ourselves, never beholding the
  Face
Whence is oblivion of self, and victory crowning
  the race.

O that the light might break, revealing the infinite
  day;
Out from its bars and its bounds the spirit would fly
  away.

He paused awhile, nor reasoned more
  Upon his bed of night;
He ceased to hear about 'him roar
  The nether infinite.
For thro' the casement blazed the sun,
  Green fields with song were rife;
With maddening abstractions done,
  He waked once more to—life.

UNCONSCIOUS INFLUENCE.

NONE OF US LIVETH TO HIMSELF.

What can it be to thee, sweet maid,
  What can it be to thee,
That ever and aye by night and day
  Thy face is the face I see?

A flower art thou upspringing
  From thine own place of birth,
And hidden fragrance bringing
  From sunshine, dew, and earth:
That the odour should go stealing
  To one who wanders by,
And fill his soul with feeling
  That knows not how to die—
What can it be to thee, sweet maid,
  What can it be to thee?

A walk and talk when earth was gay,
  No matter where nor when,
Nor whether alone we took our way
  By ocean, lake, or glen,
A walk and talk, no slighter link
  Between two souls can be,
To thee it was a glow-worm blink,
  It shines a star on me.

We never shall meet again, sweet maid,
  We never shall meet again,
But this old world about me
  Is a new world since then.
Upon it shines a glory
  That was not wont to shine:
Behind it lies a story
  I used not to divine:
Within it works a leaven
  That wrought not there before:
Above it gleams a heaven
  I did not see of yore.
All this how I detected
  At least touch of thy power,
Not even hast thou suspected—
  Unconscious as a flower.
Unconscious as a flower, sweet maid,
  Unconscious as a flower.

Moses came down from the mount of dread
  Nor wist his face did shine,
No man can live to himself, 'tis said—
And well may this thought be thine, sweet maid,
  Yea let this thought be thine.

THE CURATE'S LOVE.

HE HATH MADE EVERYTHING BEAUTIFUL IN ITS SEASON

To me my love is fair, I know,
    Yet why is she so fair?
Her brow is not so white as snow,
    Nor golden gleams her hair.
Her cheeks are not like roses giv'n
    To earth, when June is here,
And scarce so bright as June's blue heav'n
    Do her blue eyes appear.

She came when faith was all but gone
    Amid life's storm and stress;
Straightway my spirit leaned upon
    Her restful gentleness.
Since when, should she be near, I feel
    As holy ground I trod,
To me her face and form reveal
    The tenderness of God.

DON JUAN

ON

SIR WALTER SCOTT'S QUATRAIN
TO WOMAN.

TO THEM THAT ARE DEFILED AND UNBELIEVING,
NOTHING IS PURE.

I found Don Juan old and vain;
With zest he told me gallant Scott
Frankly confessed, when racked with pain,
Woman as sick nurse pleased him not.
To clinch his point he quoted next
His version of Sir Walter's text:
"O woman in our hours of ease
So fickle, coy, and hard to please,
But when disease invades the brow
What fiend so loud and hard as thou?"
With no faith left in man or woman,
The Don, I thought, ceased to be human.
Man is not man until he borrow
Wisdom from some revealing sorrow
To recognise the pure and holy
In men and women, high or lowly,
And contemplate with knightly mind
The sword of spirit in mankind.
Call ye him man who sits at ease
With that sword sleeping on his knees?
Torn from its scabbard, let him wield
A sword that flashes on God's field,
So shall he find himself again
Akin to God and godlike men.

SONG.

THOU HAST MADE SUMMER.

Springtime is over, summer is here,
Beeches are leafy, swallows appear:
Blue is the welkin, pleasant the light,
Sweetly the thrush sings, branch-hid from sight.

Voices are calling, maiden, to you,
Some one is waiting, eager to woo;
Passion of loving stirs in the air,
What beside loving merits a care?

Down by the river where the path goes
Under a bank where violet blows,
Were it not pleasant, maiden, to walk,
Pleasant to meet, and pleasant to talk?

What if his voice should whisper the word
Never forgotten once it is heard?
Word that shall fuse two lives into one—
What can compare with it under the sun?

OLD AGE AND YOUTH BY THE SEA.

AND THERE WAS NO MORE SEA.

They sat them on the beach,
Old age and frolic youth,
Together by the sea,
The boundless summer sea.

Her venerable face
Wore that tranquility
Which beautifies old age;
Her mind was far withdrawn
From the exultant joy
That sparkled on the deep.
She heeded not the kiss,
The long and lingering kiss
With which the impassioned tide
Caressed the shore, so swift
To clasp, to unclasp so slow.
The colour, sound and rhythm
Of voiceful ocean waves
Were lost on her—too old
To see, too old to hear,
Too old, too old to feel.

Elate, his youthful voice
Broke out in eager praise
Of the wide lordly main.

" Name not the sea to me,"
She cried, with sudden blaze
Of vehement protest,
Her face aglow, her mind
Alert, alive, aware,
In all its kindled depths—
" Name not the sea," she cried,
" The cruel, hateful sea,
That stabs me to the heart,
Still stabs me to the heart."

Amazement hushed his voice,
Silence fell touched with awe.
As one recalls a dream
On waking, bit by bit,
So, slowly, he recalled
A tale he once had heard
Of her two boys, who sailed
Southward, long, long ago,
And nevermore returned.
It came back like a dream
Dreamt in some far-off night,
Dimly, long, long ago.

Her venerable face
Subsided into calm,
Wore that tranquility
Which beautifies old age.
Who could suspect the rage
Deep hid within her heart
Against the lordly sea?
Or fancy she should cry
With sudden blaze of wrath
Across such length of years,
"Name not the sea to me,
The cruel, hateful sea
That stabs me to the heart,
Still stabs me to the heart."

DE PROFUNDIS.

FROM THE HORNS OF THE WILD OXEN THOU HAST
ANSWERED ME.

Lost! lost! lost!
A record stained,
A crown ungained,
The Daystar of salvation waned.

Hope! hope! hope!
Seen is the stain
And crown to gain:
Doth not the Daystar yet remain?

Were it sheer night,
Without one star
Raying from far
Bright beams to show
Thine evil plight,
And let thee know
Thy shame and woe,
Then were thy stain
And crown to gain
Quite hid from sight.

Let this sustain
Thy hope on earth—
Sense of the chain
Is freedom's birth.
That sense doth check
The prince of air,
And break the neck
Of Giant Despair.

Hope! hope! hope!
While there is light
To show the night,
To see the stain
And crown to gain,
And fetter on thy soul remain,
The Daystar shines, nor shines in vain:
Hope! hope! hope!

TO MY SISTER AGNES WHEN SAILING TO THE MISSION FIELD IN THE ZENANAS OF MADRAS.

MAKE DISCIPLES OF ALL THE NATIONS.

Light of the home who art faring
Over the sundering sea,
Home hearts with thy heart are sharing
Joy in the joy that shall be.

Daughter of morn, on the waters,
Promise of gladdening day
Breaking on India's daughters
Girds thee with song on thy way.

Midnight, or twilight, is keeping
Glory of dawn from their eyes;
Christ in their heart is but sleeping,
Lo, at their call He will rise.

Letting divine revelation
  Shine through His own, is His plan;
Healing for every nation
  Cometh through woman and man.

Sister, fair breezes attend thee!
  Speed to the work of thy choice!
Lorn hearts that loving thee lend thee,
  Elect in lending, rejoice.

TO THE SAME.

IN MEMORIAM.

Sister, a waft of fragrance from the sea
Quickens remembrance of our youth in me;
The past arises, like a dream from sleep,
Wakened by voiceful murmur of the deep.
Behold the sea-wall, net-hung as of yore,
Close to the kirk midmost the pier-lined shore.
Ah, sister dear, I see thee standing there,
A glint of sunshine on thy golden hair,
Watching with me the fishing boats from far
Draw nearer, till the brown sails cross a bar
Of crimsoned water, in the sunset hour,
Beyond the three piers and Martello Tower.
How eagerly we named each boat we knew,
Sailed proudly by its skipper and his crew!
I see the brave bronzed faces now through tears
And feel the heart-throb of our sea-girt years.
Dost thou remember too the net-hung wall,
And kirk yet hallowed by the Master's call,
And still hear, leaning from eternity,
The vast and voiceful murmur of the sea?

HYMNS.

CHRISTMAS HYMN.

THE PEOPLE THAT WALKED IN DARKNESS HAVE
SEEN A GREAT LIGHT.

Everlasting God, we bless Thee
  For Thy word and image bright,
In Whom Thine eternal purpose
  Dawned on pilgrims of the night.

Far from Thee our footsteps wandered
  On dark paths of sin and shame,
But the midnight turned to morning
  When the Lord of glory came.

Word incarnate, God-revealing,
  Longed for while dim ages ran,
Love divine, we bow before Thee,
  Son of God; and Son of man.

Let our life be new-created,
  Ever-living Lord, in Thee,
Till we wake with Thy pure likeness
  When Thy face in heaven we see:

Where the saints of all the ages,
  Where our fathers glorified,
Clouds and darkness far beneath them,
  In unending day abide.

God and Father, now we bless Thee
  For Thy word and image bright,
In Whom Thy most loving purpose
  Dawns on our adoring sight.

EASTER HYMN.

BY MAN CAME THE RESURRECTION OF THE DEAD.

From our grave hath Christ arisen
  To the Throne of God above;
Justice, wisdom, power eternal
  Are but ministers of love.
Angel hosts in strength excelling,
  Cherubim and seraphim,
Mighty thrones and strong dominions,
  He is risen, worship Him.

In Christ crucified and reigning
  God in Man hath set men free,
Free from sin's dark death and terror;
  Captive is captivity.
Herein know we God the Father;
  Grace is reigning and shall reign;
Glory, majesty, and honour
  To the Lamb that hath been slain.

Tell it to the warring peoples,—
  Jesus died and rose for all;
At the Cross of God our Brother
  Our inhuman weapons fall.
Tell the great emancipation,
  Till each ransomed heart and land
Kiss God's reconciling sceptre
  Wielded by a human hand.

123

HOLY COMMUNION.

I AM THE BREAD OF LIFE.

Our Father, in the seal and in the sign
  Of love that bled from sin to set man free,
Presented in this holy Bread and Wine,
  May we behold, may we receive from Thee
The Life of life, Who is the Light of men
To lead Thy lost ones home to Thee again.

Forgive our sin, our failure in the strife;
  Work in us Thy good pleasure to fulfil,
That, one with our inseparable Life,
  With gladness we may do and bear Thy will
In all things, with acceptance in Thine eyes
Through our Redeemer's cross and sacrifice.

We pray to Thee, O Spirit, Light, and Love,
  Father and God of Jesus Christ our Lord,
Who ever lives and reigns with Thee above,
  Upholding all things by His mighty word,
That Thou, with Him, wilt make us Thine abode,
Dwelling in us that we may dwell in God.

Members of Thy dear family of faith,
  And of the Body whereof Christ is Head,
Keep us, our Father, from all sin and scathe,
  Joyful and nourished by the Wine and Bread:
Until He come, and earth with heaven adore
The Lamb enthroned in glory evermore.

THE MINISTRY OF ANGELS.

ARE THEY NOT ALL MINISTERING SPIRITS?

What time the enemy is near
Heed not the voice that whispers fear,
　Lift up your heart on high:
The prince of darkness is in thrall
To Christ our Lord, Who saw him fall
　As lightning from the sky.

Behold your King at God's right hand:
Swift radiant hosts about Him stand,
　His bidding to fulfil;
These holy myriads ever share
The glory of His perfect care
　For all who do His will.

He cannot fail who truly boasts
A Leader in the Lord of hosts,
　For evermore the same;
Over the power of death and sin
Great triumph shall His servants win
　Who battle in His Name.

Clad in His armour take the field,
Be hope your helmet, faith your shield,
　Your allies hosts of heaven;
Fell is the fight, but not for long,
Soon shall you share their victor song
　To whom the crown is given.

HYMN BEFORE BATTLE.

RENDER UNTO CÆSAR THE THINGS THAT ARE CÆSAR'S.

Pity us, our Father, when
    Brothers still with brothers fight;
Hear us when we plead again—
    "God defend the right."

Though Thou slay us, O our God,
    We believe our cause is just,
And our blood shall from the clod
    Witness to our trust.

Sinful, mortal, yet there burns
    Light in us Thy Spirit gives:
When our dust to dust returns
    Thy life in us lives.

Speed the coming of the day
    When on earth all war shall cease:
Though it halt and long delay
    There shall yet be peace.

While these days of trouble last
    Homes are sad and full of care;
On Thy Fatherhood we cast
    All, and leave them there.

When her sons from war retire
    May the motherland rejoice;
Let her after storm and fire
    Hear Thy still small voice.

THE FINAL VISION.

THE LIGHT OF THE KNOWLEDGE OF THE GLORY OF GOD IN THE FACE OF JESUS CHRIST.

Up, up, my soul, thy flight is not yet o'er,
Thy resting place is high, still must thou soar;
Droop not thy wing, look up, pour forth thy song,
Soar up, soar on, thou wilt alight ere long;
And then thine hour of welcoming will come
To love, joy, peace, in thine appointed home.

Up, up, my soul, the stars thou dost not see
Set not, but move in steadfast harmony;
What though the mist be chill, and dark the night?
Soar up, soar on, till in the hard-won height
The day shall dawn upon the city dear,
Where hope no longer needs to lighten fear.

Up, up, my soul, thy strength abideth still,
Rooted in His revealed eternal will:
The hidden Presence girdeth thee about,
Soar up, soar on, to see, not from without
But from within at last, the holy place,
And that great light in our Redeemer's face.

IN HOC SIGNO VICTOR.

WE FLY AWAY.

Out of life
Into death,
Moses said,
We fly away.
Fly away! saints have thought this word points
To the Cross—Flying birds cleave the air
Cruciform—
Living signs
All may see
Of the faith.
We fly away.
Even so
In this sign
Conquerors.

CARLISLE: CHAS THURNAM & SONS, PRINTERS, 11 ENGLISH STREET.

CPSIA information can be obtained
at www.ICGtesting.com
Printed in the USA
BVHW071112160819
556065BV00003B/98/P